THE PYRAMIDS

**EGYPT
POCKET
GUIDE**

Alberto Siliotti

THE AMERICAN UNIVERSITY IN CAIRO PRESS

Text and Photographs Alberto Siliotti
Drawings Stefania Cossu
English Translation Richard Pierce

General Editing Yvonne Marzoni
Graphic Design Geodia

Copyright © 2002 by Geodia (Verona, Italy)

This edition first published in Egypt jointly by
The American University in Cairo Press (Cairo and New York)
Elias Modern Publishing House (Cairo)
Geodia (Verona, Italy)

Created by Geodia (Verona, Italy)
Printed in Egypt by Elias Modern Publishing House (Cairo)
Distributed by the American University in Cairo Press (Cairo and New York)

ISBN 977 424 640 3   Dar el Kutub No. 17879/00

Contents

The Pyramid of Khafre

King Menkaure

The tomb of Meresankh at Giza

Sunset at Giza

CHRONOLOGICAL TABLE

3200 B.C.–2920 B.C.	**PREDYNASTIC**
2920 B.C.–2635 B.C.	**EARLY DYNASTIC** Dynasty 0 / 1st Dynasty / 2nd Dynasty
2635 B.C.–2140 B.C.	**OLD KINGDOM**

3rd DYNASTY from 2635 B.C. to 2561 B.C.
Sanakhte
Djoser (Horus Netjerikhet)
Horus Sekhemkhet
Khaba
Huni

4th DYNASTY from 2561 B.C. to 2450 B.C.
Snofru
Khufu (Cheops)
Djedefre
Khafre (Chephren)
Menkaure (Mycerinus)
Shepseskaf

5th DYNASTY from 2450 B.C. to 2321 B.C.
Userkaf
Sahure
Neferirkara
Shepseskare
Neferefre
Nyuserre
Menkhauhor
Djedkare-Isesi
Unas

6th DYNASTY from 2321 B.C. to 2140 B.C.
Teti
Pepy I
Merenra
Pepy II

GIZA
Khufu
Khafre
Menkaure

CAIRO

TURA

ZAWIYET AL-ARYAN — Khaba

Niuserre's Sun Temple
Userkaf's Sun Temple
ABUSIR
Sahure
Neferirkara
Nyuserra

ABUSIR

Teti
Userkaf
Djoser
Unas
Sekhemkhet
Pepy I
SAQQARA
Merenra
Djedkare-Isesi
Pepy II
Al-Fara'un Mastaba (Shepseskaf)
Khendjer

MIT-RAHINA
Memphis

SAQQARA

HELWAN

Senwosret III
Snofru
Amenemhet II
DAHSHUR
Snofru
Amenemhet III
Pyramid of Mazghuna

DAHSHUR

MEIDUM

N

The Pyramids   5

The History

*T*he pyramids, and the great pyramids of Giza in particular, have always aroused admiration and awe, as they are the expression of a civilization which had already in the 3rd millennium B.C. achieved a remarkable level of technological development.

The hieroglyph mer, *which means 'pyramid'*

The pyramids of Giza

Built around the middle of the 3rd millennium B.C. at the fringe of a desert plateau that has been partly overrun by the southern outskirts of Cairo, the great pyramids of Giza have stirred the imagination of travelers, historians, geographers, scientists, artists, and all the others who have had the good fortune to admire them first-hand. Of the famous Seven Wonders of the Ancient World, the pyramids of Giza are the only ones that have managed to withstand time and remain intact to this day, at the dawn of the 3rd millennium A.D. Thousands of books have been written about the pyramids and many varied and fanciful theories have been set forth regarding their construction: medieval Arab historians related that the ancient Egyptians had the power to annul the force of gravity, while in more recent times some persons have claimed that the pyramids bear the 'imprints of the gods' and

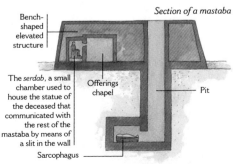

Section of a mastaba

Bench-shaped elevated structure

The *serdab*, a small chamber used to house the statue of the deceased that communicated with the rest of the mastaba by means of a slit in the wall

Offerings chapel

Pit

Sarcophagus

are the vestiges of an extremely ancient, unknown civilization, a well-spring of the Great Initiates' esoteric wisdom. Indeed, the pyramids of Giza exude such an aura of mystery and power and are so awe-inspiring that one's imagination exceeds all reasonable bounds. The pyramids, called *mer* by the ancient Egyptians, were the result of evolution–both philosophical and technological–that lasted several centuries. The

The al-Fara'un mastaba at Saqqara

history, the so-called **Step Pyramid**, in the **Saqqara** necropolis. Imhotep conceived a sort of symbolic staircase that would allow the pharaoh's

Djoser's Step Pyramid at Saqqara

mastabas, the simplest and most common monumental tombs of the Old Kingdom, consisted of a pit or trench in which the sarcophagus was placed, and external casing that made the construction look like a large bench, hence the Arabic word *mastaba*. It was the pharaoh Djoser's great architect and vizier Imhotep who, at the beginning of the 3rd Dynasty, around 2600 B.C., got the idea of elevating the mastaba of his sovereign and created the first **pyramid** in

soul to ascend to heaven. The theological concepts that held sway in this period considered the pharaoh divine: he was the son of the sun-god Re and the intermediary between the sky and earth who ensured prosperity to his land. Further evolution in Egyptian thought and

building techniques then led to certain intermediate types such as the **pyramid of Meidum** and the **Bent Pyramid of Dahshur**, and finally to the true pyramid. Built with large limestone blocks quarried on the spot, the pyramids were then dressed with slabs of fine, smooth, white Tura limestone that was extracted in the quarries at Tura on the eastern bank of the Nile, a few kilometers south of Giza. The pyramids were then crowned with a capstone known as a *pyramidion*, which was sometimes dressed with a thin sheet

Satellite pyramid

Causeway

Valley temple

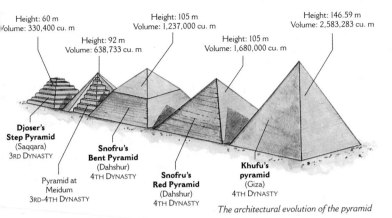

Height: 60 m
Volume: 330,400 cu. m

Height: 92 m
Volume: 638,733 cu. m

Height: 105 m
Volume: 1,237,000 cu. m

Height: 105 m
Volume: 1,680,000 cu. m

Height: 146.59 m
Volume: 2,583,283 cu. m

**Djoser's
Step Pyramid**
(Saqqara)
3RD DYNASTY

Pyramid at
Meidum
3RD-4TH DYNASTY

**Snofru's
Bent Pyramid**
(Dahshur)
4TH DYNASTY

**Snofru's
Red Pyramid**
(Dahshur)
4TH DYNASTY

**Khufu's
pyramid**
(Giza)
4TH DYNASTY

The architectural evolution of the pyramid

of *electrum*, an alloy of gold and silver that reflected the rays of the sun onto the plain below. Thus, the pyramids, with their smooth, shiny surfaces, were the symbolic materialization of the sun's rays.

Other monumental elements were part of the pyramid complex, each of which had its own specific function: the mortuary temple, the causeway, the valley temple, and the satellite pyramid.

The **mortuary temple**, usually situated on the east side of the pyramid, was the site where the ceremonies of the cult of the dead, divinized pharaoh took place, while the **valley temple**, built at the edge of a basin that was connected to the Nile via secondary canals and to the mortuary temple by a **causeway**, temporarily housed the body of the dead pharaoh. Egyptologists think the actual embalming took place in either special mobile structures in the immediate vicinity or inside the valley temple itself. On the south side of the pyramid there might be a small **'satellite' pyramid** that most probably represented the tomb of the *ka*, the immaterial double of the pharaoh. Sometimes other smaller pyramids were added to the complex—the **subsidiary pyramids** for the royal consort.

Mortuary temple

Pyramidion

N

Enclosure wall

Storehouses

Courtyard

The funerary complex consisted of the pyramid and the architectural substructures: the mortuary temple, the causeway, and the valley temple, which stood on the bank of a basin connected to the Nile and was used to temporarily house the remains of the pharaoh

The pyramidion *on the pyramid of Amenemhet III at Dahshur
(Egyptian Museum, Cairo)*

The Building Technique

*T*he ancient
Egyptians
were quite
knowledgeable
about
astronomy,
mathematics,
and
architecture,
and they made
extraordinary
achievements in
construction
despite the
rather simple
apparatuses
they used.

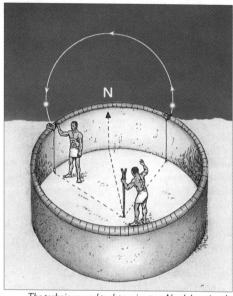

The technique used to determine true North by using the merkhet, a gauge that measured the position of a circumpolar star when it rose and set

*T*he techniques employed to build the pyramids and lift the huge blocks of limestone—which on an average weighed around 2.5 tons—to heights of over 100 meters, remain a mystery, since no evidence has come down to us. The great Greek historian Herodotus, who visited Egypt in the 5th century B.C., two thousand years after the construction of the pyramids, speaks at length of these monuments in the second book of *The Histories*, but in this regard says merely that the blocks were hoisted by machines made of short timbers. The various theories concerning the construction techniques speak of the creation of specially made ramps, either straight or 'spiral,' with an inclination that allowed workers to drag the huge blocks, which were placed on wooden

A

Reconstruction of the merkhet, which was used to determine the height of a star on the horizon. It consisted of a level with a plumb line (A) and a forked rod (B) that allowed experts to spot the star

B

A square level with a plumb line (Egyptian Museum, Cairo)

sledges. On the other hand, the rudimentary but quite functional tools used by the laborers and craftsmen are well known. They included wooden mallets, bronze or copper chisels, squares, and plumb lines. The ancient Egyptians' knowledge of mathematics and geometry was quite advanced, enabling architects to build colossal works with astonishing precision. For example, the sides of the Pyramid of Khufu, which are about 230 meters long, differ less than five centimeters in length, and the astronomical orientation of this monument is only three minutes, six seconds of arc away from true North.

Herodotus writes that 100,000 laborers, mostly slaves, were forced to work in inhuman conditions, goaded by cruel guards, in order to satisfy the ambition of a despotic and megalomanic sovereign. But modern archaeology and Egyptology provide a quite different picture. The pyramids were built by artisans and specialized workers who received regular wages, while the manual labor was done by farmers in the summer, when the Nile River was flooded and they could not work. On the whole, there must have been about 20,000–30,000 such laborers.

The tools used to shape limestone blocks (Egyptian Museum, Cairo)

This statuette of Inti-shedu "overseer of the bark of Neith" was recently discovered in the workmen's cemetery of Giza by the famous archaeologist Zahi Hawass (Egyptian Museum, Cairo)

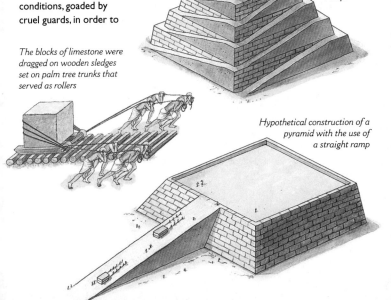

Hypothetical construction of a pyramid with the use of spiral ramps

The blocks of limestone were dragged on wooden sledges set on palm tree trunks that served as rollers

Hypothetical construction of a pyramid with the use of a straight ramp

Giza

*T*he most
famous and
popular
Memphite
necropolis is the
one at Giza, on
the outskirts of
Cairo, with its
three great
pyramids and
the mysterious
Sphinx.

The Great Sphinx is a symbol of ancient Egypt

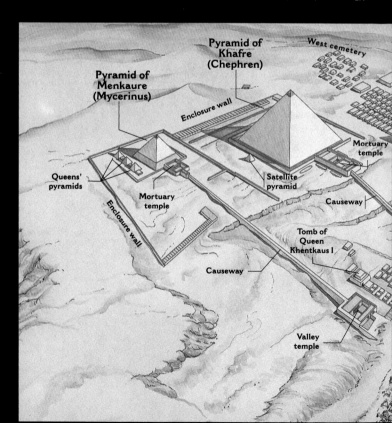

Pyramid of
Khafre
(Chephren)

West cemetery

Pyramid of
Menkaure
(Mycerinus)

Enclosure wall

Mortuary
temple

Queens'
pyramids

Satellite
pyramid

Enclosure wall

Mortuary
temple

Causeway

Tomb of
Queen
Khentkaus I

Causeway

Valley
temple

It was Khufu (*Cheops*), the son of Snofru, who inaugurated the necropolis of Giza, which in ancient times was called Rosetau, situated on a desert plateau that is now surrounded to the north and east by the southern quarters of Cairo. In antiquity the Giza plateau lay in the immediate vicinity of the Nile, to which it was connected via a network of canals and basins that washed the causeways of the valley temples of the pyramids. Thousands of persons—workmen, artisans, and artists—lived on this site, whose structures were recently discovered. At Giza, Khufu built the largest pyramid in the world. His example was followed by two of his successors, Khafre (*Chephren*) and Menkaure (*Mycerinus*), thus increasing the fame of Giza, the pyramids of which were considered one of the Seven Wonders of the Ancient World. In more recent times the necropolis of Giza was made part of UNESCO's Heritage of Humanity list. The new Egyptian Museum will be built a short distance from the archaeological area of Giza and will house the most important objects now on display in the present-day museum in Cairo.

Detail of the diorite statue of Khafre discovered in the valley temple (Egyptian Museum, Cairo)

The Giza necropolis in 2400 B.C.

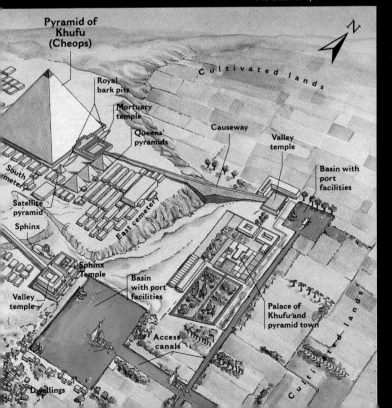

Pyramid of Khufu (Cheops)

Cultivated lands

Royal bark pits

Mortuary temple

Causeway

Queens' pyramids

Valley temple

Basin with port facilities

South cemetery

Satellite pyramid

Sphinx

East cemetery

Sphinx Temple

Basin with port facilities

Valley temple

Palace of Khufu and pyramid town

Access canals

Dwellings

Cultivated lands

The Pyramid of Khufu

*T*he largest monument in four thousand years of Egyptian history, the Pyramid of Khufu was built in a twenty-year period by 20,000–30,000 workmen.

The cartouche of Khufu (Cheops)

The Pyramid of Khufu

Khufu, whom the ancient Greeks called *Cheops*, was the pharaoh who succeeded

This ivory statuette from Abydos (7.6 cm) is the only existing image of Khufu (Egyptian Museum, Cairo)

Snofru, the founder of the 4th Dynasty who built two large pyramids in the Dahshur necropolis, about twenty kilometers south of Giza. The Pyramid of Khufu is the oldest one at Giza and is so large it could contain St. Peter's Basilica in Rome. Napoleon, who was a mathematics enthusiast, calculated that the blocks of stone used to build this

colossal monument would have been enough to erect a wall two meters high and 30 centimeters thick all around France. Because of an optical illusion created by the different inclination of the faces of the three

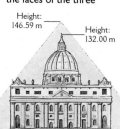

Height: 146.59 m

Height: 132.00 m

The Pyramid of Khufu with St. Peter's 'inside'

pyramids at Giza and by the different ground level, one gets the impression that the Pyramid of Khafre (built on a slightly elevated position) is the largest; however, the Pyramid of Khufu is actually larger than any other. Over 2,500,000 blocks of stone, with an average weight of 2.5 tons, extracted at a quarry only a few hundred meters south of the pyramid itself, and about 20,000–30,000 workmen were needed to build this colossal structure. Since the first official act of a pharaoh was to announce the beginning of work on the construction of his tomb, and since Khufu reigned for about 23 years, it must have taken at least 20 years to build this monument.

As for the date when work on the pyramid began, an English scholar recently theorized that it was oriented on the basis of the alignment of two stars, Kochab and Mizar, which, according to his calculations, occurred in 2467 B.C. The deviation of three minutes from true North was supposedly not the result of an error in calculation but rather due to the actual cyclical movement these two stars describe, a movement that lasts 26,000 years. Bearing in mind this deviation, the pyramid would have been built in 2478 B.C., 76 years earlier than the

The Ursa Major and Ursa Minor constellations, with the stars Mizar and Kochab

traditional date ascribed to the pyramid, while those of Khafre and Menkaure were probably built in 2446 and 2413 B.C. respectively.

It is not clear what led Khufu to abandon Dahshur, the site his father Snofru had chosen

---

THE PYRAMID IN FIGURES

Original height: 146.59 m
Actual height: 139.75 m
Base length: 230.33 m
Angle of slope: 51° 50' 47"
Total volume: 2,583,283 cu. m
Number of blocks used: 2,300,000
Average size of blocks: 1 x 1 x 1 m
Average weight of blocks: 2.5 tons

$\alpha = 51° 50' 47"$

The Pyramid of Khufu (Cheops), whose original name was Akhet-Khufu, or 'the horizon of Khufu,' has always fascinated not only mathematicians and scholars, such as the great Egyptologist Sir William M. Flinders Petrie or the astronomer Charles Piazzi Smith, but also the many enthusiasts who love to fantasize about archaeology because of the extraordinary mathematical ratios governing the construction, which attest to the high level of knowledge attained by the Egyptians in the 3rd millennium B.C. The ratio of the AB apothem and half of the side of each face is equal to the famous 'golden section' (so named because it corresponds to a ratio considered the best from an aesthetic standpoint), which corresponds to 1.618 and which in turn determines the 51° 50' angle of slope of the faces: this is also the only angle whose tangent is equal to the inverse of its sine. Furthermore, the perimeter of the base of the pyramid is equal to the circumference of a circle whose radius corresponds exactly to its height.

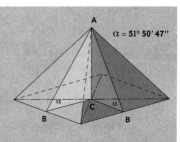

the inner chambers were built in keeping with a complex plan that called for innovative technical and architectural

The original entrance to the pyramid

as his eternal abode, in favor of Rosetau, as the necropolis of Giza was called at that time, but religious motives certainly played a role here. Once the ideal site was chosen on the basis of astronomers' calculations, the pharaoh's architects had a basin excavated and fitted with a pier and other port facilities. A canal connected this with the Nile so that building material could be transported from distant quarries, and a causeway (remains of which were recently discovered) was built to connect the basin and the pyramid

construction area. Other teams of workmen extracted limestone from a deposit a few hundred meters south of Giza and then cut the large blocks of stone that would constitute the core of the structure. As the pyramid grew in height,

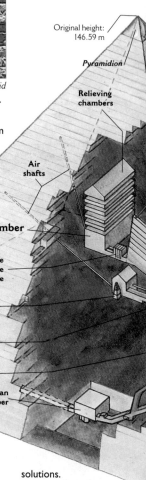

Original height: 146.59 m

Pyramidion

Relieving chambers

Air shafts

King's chamber

Granite portcullis closure device

Queen's chamber

Horizontal passageway

Secondary shaft

Subterranean chamber

solutions.
The **ascending passageway** after the entrance leads to the so-called **Grand Gallery**, with angled, corbeled walls, which is considered a masterpiece of ancient architecture. This in turn gives access to the **pharaoh's burial chamber**, the entrance of which was protected

The pharaoh's sarcophagus

by a granite portcullis closure system. The pharaoh's chamber, which housed the sarcophagus, was built with gigantic blocks of red granite from Aswan, over 600 kilometers south of Giza. For the first time in the history of ancient Egyptian architecture the ceiling of this chamber was flat, and not a pitched

the structure from collapsing. Besides the king's burial chamber, the pyramid had two other underground chambers: the so-called **queen's chamber**, which probably housed a statue of the royal *ka* (the immaterial double of the deceased king), and the **subterranean chamber**, hewn out of the rock of the Giza plateau under the foundation of the pyramid itself, which may have symbolized the abode of the god Sokar. Two tunnels, improperly called

The Grand Gallery

constellation and the circumpolar stars, which served to facilitate the heavenly ascent of the pharaoh's soul. The pyramid was then covered with slabs of white Tura limestone; this casing managed to endure the ravages of time, but not of humanity. The limestone slabs remained almost intact up to the Middle Ages, but were then removed from the pyramid and used as building material for mosques and other buildings in Cairo.

air shafts, started off from the king's and queen's chambers; they were aligned with the Orion

Air shafts

Grand Gallery

Ascending passageway

Entrance

Length: 230.33 m

Descending passageway

The interior of the Pyramid of Khufu

vault, and it was made of blocks weighing over 70 tons. Over this the architects built a complex network of empty spaces known as **relieving chambers** to prevent

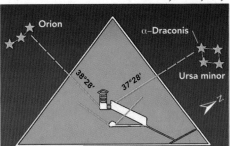

Astronomical orientation of the so-called air shafts in the Pyramid of Khufu

Orion

α–Draconis

Ursa minor

38°28'

37°28'

The Royal Bark

Khufu's royal bark, which was found intact after 4,500 years, illustrates the high level of naval technology attained in Egypt in the 3rd millennium B.C.

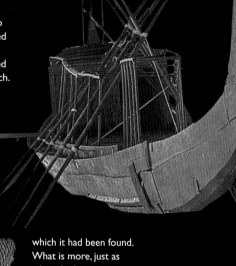

In 1954 archaeologists discovered, on the southern side of the Pyramid of Khufu, two pits hermetically sealed with large blocks of limestone that weighed about twenty tons each. The eastern pit was opened. It contained a splendid boat entirely dismantled in 1,224 pieces of Lebanese cedarwood. Thanks to

The bark's mooring rope is in a perfect state of preservation

which it had been found. What is more, just as when the boat was originally constructed, this operation was carried out without using a single nail or other metal piece, as hemp ropes were used in an ingenious system to put the planking together.

painstaking work that lasted fourteen years, in 1968 the boat was reassembled in a museum built especially to house it, a few meters from the pit in

Detail of the system of fastening the oars

Five pairs of oars

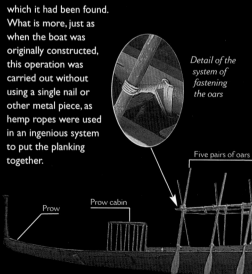

Prow

Prow cabin

Ahmed Yussef restored the royal bark

The royal bark pits on the east side of the Pyramid of Khufu

The dismantled royal bark as it appeared when it was discovered

The boat is 43.4 meters long and 5.6 meters wide and was used for river navigation, as can be seen by its slight draft. It was and pillaged already in antiquity—that originally contained one boat each. Most probably these boats had a symbolic meaning: just as the sun god Re

The planking of the boat with its frames

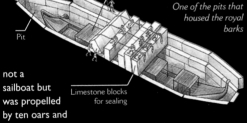

One of the pits that housed the royal barks

not a sailboat but was propelled by ten oars and steered by a double stern rudder.

The bark belonged to a fleet that was part of the pharaoh's funerary equipment. On the east side of the pyramid are five large pits—opened crossed the sky every day aboard his solar boat, the pharaoh's soul joined his divine father and navigated with him in eternity.

THE ROYAL BARK IN FIGURES

Length 43.4 m
Width 5.9 m
Draft 1.5 m
Displacement 45 tons

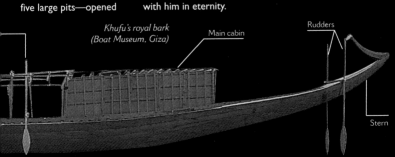

Khufu's royal bark (Boat Museum, Giza)

The Pyramid of Khafre

The cartouche of Khafre (Chephren)

*T*he second pyramid at Giza, built by Khafre, one of Khufu's sons, is the only one on which the original Tura limestone casing is intact, although only on the top.

The Pyramid of Khafre

*T*he son and successor of Khufu, **Djedefre**, decided to abandon the site his father had chosen as his eternal abode and had his pyramid built in an isolated place about eight kilometers northwest of Giza that is now known as Abu

The diorite statue of Khafre that Auguste Mariette found in the valley temple (Egyptian Museum, Cairo)

The three pyramids at Giza

Rawash. **Khafre**, Khufu's other son, who succeeded Djedefre and was called *Chephren* by the ancient Greeks, decided to return to Giza and have his pyramid built southwest of his father's. Although Khafre's pyramid is three meters shorter than Khufu's, at first sight it seems to be taller because of its slightly

elevated position (about ten meters) and because its sides are more inclined (53° 10' as opposed to 51° 50' 47"). Up to the 19th century people believed Herodotus' affirmation that this pyramid had no inner chambers. The great Italian explorer and

The pharaoh's sarcophagus

Giovanni Belzoni

traveler from Padua, Giovanni Belzoni, had his doubts and set about searching for the pyramid entrance, which he found on March 2, 1818.

chamber. It is not clear whether this arrangement was due to a change in the original building project or whether this underground chamber had a symbolic function much like the one in Khufu's pyramid.

The **burial chamber**, which is reached by means of an upper descending passageway that then proceeds horizontally, consists of large granite slabs and measures 70.75 square meters, sixteen square meters more than

Khufu's burial chamber. Outside, on the east side of the pyramid, are the remains of the grandiose **mortuary temple**, made of gigantic blocks

Khafre's mortuary temple

of granite (the largest of which weighs about 400 tons). The temple was originally 110 meters long, but since it was used for centuries as an open-air 'quarry' for building material, its appearance is obviously different from the original.

The inscription made by Belzoni to certify his discovery

The mortuary chambers in the Pyramid of Khafre are much simpler than those in Khufu's. They include a **burial chamber** containing the pharaoh's granite sarcophagus, and an **unfinished underground chamber**

connected to the outside by a passageway that is also connected to the upper passageway leading to the burial

Interior of the Pyramid of Khafre

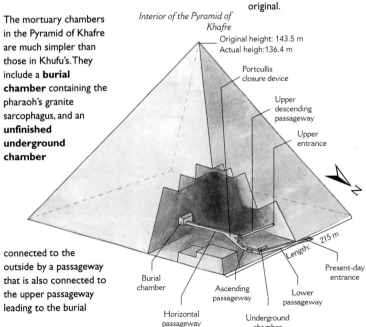

Original height: 143.5 m
Actual heigh: 136.4 m

Portcullis closure device

Upper descending passageway

Upper entrance

Length: 215 m

Present-day entrance

Burial chamber

Ascending passageway

Lower passageway

Horizontal passageway

Underground chamber (unfinished)

Khafre's Valley Temple

*B*uilt with large blocks of granite from Aswan, this
impressive monument originally housed 23
splendid diorite statues of the pharaoh.
One of them, discovered intact, is a true
masterpiece of Egyptian art.

The causeway

A causeway 494.5
meters long
connects the mortuary
temple of Khafre with his
valley temple, which was
discovered and
excavated in
1852 by the
great
Egyptologist
Auguste
Mariette,
the founder
of Cairo's
Egyptian

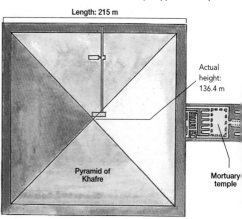

Khafre's pyramid complex

Length: 215 m

Actual height: 136.4 m

Pyramid of Khafre

Mortuary temple

*The diorite statue of Khafre
discovered in the valley temple
(Egyptian Museum, Cairo)*

Satellite pyramid

The valley temple

and is built entirely of piers and architraves made of pink granite from Aswan, while the floor is made of alabaster. Inside there were 23 statues of the pharaoh Khafre seated on his throne.

The temple had two **entrances** on its east side, each of which was preceded by a pair of sphinxes, an evocation of the pharaoh's two-part role as sovereign of Lower and Upper Egypt. The entrance corridors afford access to a longitudinal **vestibule** with walls made of large blocks of granite and the floor paved with white alabaster. The vestibule in turn leads to the T-shaped central hall. Mariette found the marvelous diorite statue of Khafre in a pit cut out of the rock in the middle of the vestibule. The sculpture, now exhibited at the Egyptian Museum, Cairo, was one of the 23 statues placed in the central hall, the only remains of which are the pedestals.

Museum. Khafre's valley temple is the only building of this type in the vast Giza necropolis that can be seen in its entirety.

The narrow corridor in the middle of the **causeway**, which originally had a roof, leads directly into the large **central hall** of the temple. This is in the shape of an inverted 'T'

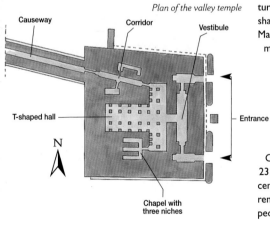

Plan of the valley temple

Causeway

Corridor

Vestibule

T-shaped hall

Entrance

N

Chapel with three niches

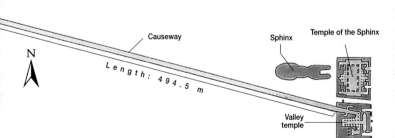

N

Causeway

L e n g t h : 4 9 4 . 5 m

Sphinx

Temple of the Sphinx

Valley temple

The Great Sphinx

*N*o other ancient Egyptian monument has stirred more admiration and interest than the *Sphinx* at Giza, which, because of its everlasting aura of mystery, has given rise to many legends and beliefs.

The Great Sphinx and the Pyramid of Khufu in the background

The Great Sphinx at Giza is probably the most famous monument of ancient Egypt and has become its symbol. Its lion's body and human head were carved out of

The Sphinx's lion's body in 22:1 scale. It was sculpted out of Tertiary Era nummulitic limestone from the so-called Muqattam Formation and dates back to about 40 million years ago

Remains of a statue probably added by Amenophis II (18th Dynasty)

Stele of Tuthmosis IV (18th Dynasty)

One-meter hole perhaps used to support a crown

Nemes headdress

Six-meter head depicting Khafre in 30:1 scale

The Sphinx

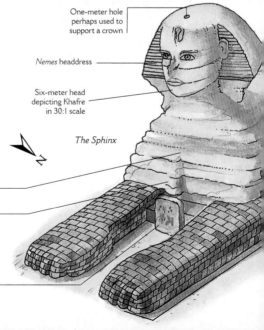

a mass of nummulitic limestone—which had previously been 'sculpted' by wind erosion—around 2500 B.C. The Sphinx was the symbolic image of the pharaoh and at the same time the guardian of the royal necropolis of Giza. During the New Kingdom the Sphinx, a word that derives from the Egyptian *seseps ankh,* or 'living idol,' was associated with the god Horemakhet (Horus of the Horizon) and later with Hurun, a god of Syrian origin. Between the Sphinx's forepaws there is a large stele known as the 'Dream Stele' that was placed there by Tuthmosis IV (18th Dynasty), who

The Sphinx with Tuthmosis IV's Dream Stele

Vertical shaft about 8.3 meters long

Height: 20 m

Vertical shaft about eight meters deep

Holes perhaps dating from the Roman period that may have been used as incense burners

Length: 74 m

was also the first to clear the monument of sand. In fact, the Sphinx was covered by sand several times up to the 19th century, and often only its head was visible. It was also restored many times, the last restoration being completed in 1998 under the supervision of the famous Egyptian Egyptologist, Zahi Hawass.

Various restorations carried out from the New Kingdom (1550–1076 B.C.) to 1998 A.D.

Detail of Tuthmosis IV's stele

The Sphinx Temple

Situated next to Khafre's valley temple, this building connected to the Great Sphinx is still a mystery for Egyptologists because no existing text mentions it.

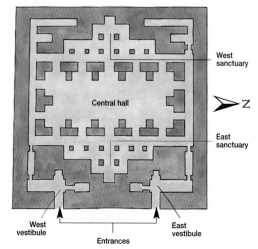

Plan of the Sphinx Temple

Much like the valley temple of Khafre, the so-called Sphinx Temple had a double entrance that gave access, via a **vestibule** consisting of two right-angle chambers, to the **central hall** with its 24 large granite piers. Of these latter, the ten centrally placed ones are much larger. On the east and west sides of the central hall there were two **sanctuaries**. The structure of the central hall is similar to that of

View of the Sphinx Temple, flanked by the small New Kingdom temple

The Sphinx Temple

the valley temple; as in the valley temple, at the base of the piers archaeologists found the pedestals of twelve large statues of the pharaoh Khafre.

The purpose and symbolic-ritual meaning of this impressive building, which is a superb example of megalithic architecture, are not known, but scholars believe the piers were related to the 24 hours of the day and that the two sanctuaries represent the solar god at dawn and sunset.

Indeed, it is probable that the entire temple was related to the solar cult, which at that time was becoming more and more important, and that its orientation had an astronomic relation to particular times of the year such as the equinox and solstice.

It is interesting to note that while the alignment of the causeway of the Pyramid of Khafre deviates 15° to the south, the alignment of the Sphinx Temple is on a perfect East-West axis, so that during the autumn and spring equinoxes the rays of the rising sun cross its central section.

This is the reason why the temple was dedicated to the god Horemakhet, 'Horus of the Horizon.'

The temple piers

Reconstruction of the Sphinx Temple and the valley temple of Khafre

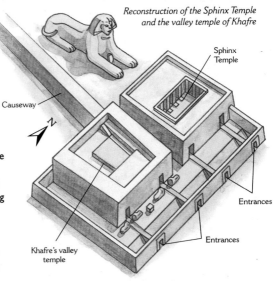

Sphinx Temple

Causeway

Entrances

Entrances

Khafre's valley temple

The Pyramid of Menkaure

The cartouche of Menkaure (or Mycerinus)

*T*he third pyramid at Giza, built by the pharaoh Menkaure, is 65 meters high and is therefore much smaller than the other two. It was opened only in 1837 by the Englishman Richard Vyse, who found the pharaoh's sarcophagus, which was then lost while being transported to England.

The Pyramid of Menkaure, with the huge hole made by Uthman in 1196

*M*ycerinus is the Greek transliteration of the name of the pharaoh **Menkaure**, who succeeded Khafre and built a pyramid much smaller than those of his two predecessors, 'only' 65 meters high and with a volume less than 1/10 of Khufu's pyramid. Menkaure's pyramid stands southwest of Khafre's. Its lower third was dressed with red granite slabs that can still be clearly seen, while the upper two-thirds had Tura limestone casing. Despite the gaping hole opened in the middle of its northern face by the caliph Uthman in 1196, this was the only pyramid that remained inviolate after the ancient period. It wasn't until 1837 that British colonel Richard Vyse and engineer John Shea Perring, after many fruitless attempts, finally succeeded in finding the entrance and went inside the monument.

The funerary chambers

Detail of one of the so-called Triads of Menkaure depicting the pharaoh (Egyptian Museum, Cairo)

Red granite slabs from the original casing of the pyramid

The interior of the pyramid

are quite complex and the presence of two descending passageways (the upper one was never finished and was then abandoned) would indicate a variation in the **horizontal passageway** that leads to the large **original burial chamber**, aligned on the East-West axis, with a surface area of 54.53 square meters. In the being transported to England in 1838. A **chamber with six niches** lies a few meters west of the burial chamber. Its use is not clear to Egyptologists, but it may have had an evocative, symbolic meaning, much like Khafre's subterranean chamber, or it may have been used to house food and offerings for the royal *ka*. On the southern side of the pyramid there are three **queen's pyramids** for the royal wives. The one furthest east (called GIIIc) is considered the tomb of Queen Khamerernebty II, although some

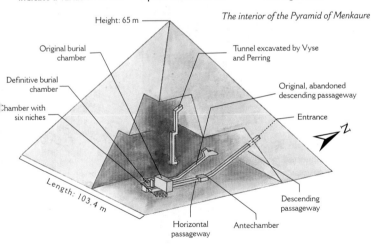

The interior of the Pyramid of Menkaure

Height: 65 m

Original burial chamber

Definitive burial chamber

Chamber with six niches

Length: 103.4 m

Tunnel excavated by Vyse and Perring

Original, abandoned descending passageway

Entrance

Descending passageway

Horizontal passageway

Antechamber

original building plans during construction. The **descending passageway** leads to an **antechamber** which, for the first time in Old Kingdom architecture, had walls decorated with false doors. This marks the beginning of a middle of this chamber is another descending passage that leads to the **definitive burial chamber**, where Vyse and Perring found a beautiful sarcophagus, decorated with a motif of a palace façade, which was lost at sea while

The lost sarcophagus of Menkaure

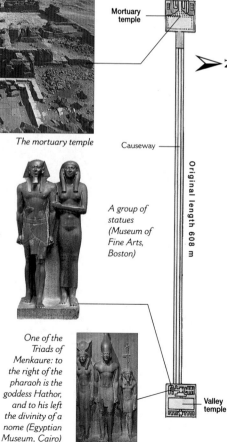

districts) of Egypt. Most probably there were about forty of these triads, one for each of the nomes. In the same section of the temple Reisner also found a splendid double statue of Menkaure and his consort Khamerernebty II, which was placed in the Museum of Fine Arts, Boston.

The Pyramid of Menkaure with the Queens' Pyramids

GIIIa
GIIIb
GIIIc

architectural elements have led archaeologists to believe that this was originally a satellite pyramid. On the eastern

The Menkaure pyramid complex

GIIIa

Queens' (secondary) pyramids — GIIIb

Pyramid of Khamerernebty II— GIIIc

Entrance

Mortuary temple

→ z

The mortuary temple

Causeway

Original length 608 m

side of the pyramid are the remains of the **mortuary temple**, which was connected by a 608–meter **causeway** to the **valley temple**, the ruins of which are buried in the sand. In 1908, during the excavation of this temple, the American archaeologist George Reisner discovered the four intact and two fragmentary *triads*, group sculptures with three figures depicting Menkaure flanked by the goddess Hathor and a divinity who personified one of the nomes (or

A group of statues (Museum of Fine Arts, Boston)

One of the Triads of Menkaure: to the right of the pharaoh is the goddess Hathor, and to his left the divinity of a nome (Egyptian Museum, Cairo)

Valley temple

The Private Tombs at Giza

Although they are not popular tourist attractions, the private tombs east and west of the Great Pyramid, decorated with sculpture and polychrome bas-reliefs, are of great artistic value and allow us to reconstruct the daily life in Egypt when the pyramids were built.

The tomb of Queen Meresankh III

To the east and west of the Pyramid of Khufu there are two large necropolises consisting of rows of mastabas in a rather orderly arrangement.

The carrying chair and gold jug of Queen Hetepheres (Egyptian Museum, Cairo)

These were the tombs of the members of the royal family and of leading officials who enjoyed the great privilege of being buried near their sovereign in order to share, to some degree, the power of resurrection that his divine nature embodied. Among the tombs on the eastern side of the pyramid, which constitute the so-called **east cemetery**, are those of the members of the royal family, while the tombs on the opposite side of the pyramid, which make up the **west cemetery**,

were mostly for high officials. In the east cemetery is the shaft tomb of **Queen Hetepheres**, Khufu's mother, which is known above all for its rich funerary equipment, now on display at the

Meresankh III

Tomb of Kaemankh: scene of a cow giving birth

Egyptian Museum, Cairo. The same cemetery also has the **tomb of Queen Meresankh III**, the grand-daughter of Khufu and Khafre's consort, famous for its sheer beauty and the polychrome bas-reliefs that decorate the walls with scenes of hunting and fishing, the preparation of food, and the creation of handicraft objects. The tomb of Meresankh is open to the

Tomb of Kaemankh: preparing food and drinks

public, as are other tombs in this cemetery: the tomb of **Qar**, who bore the title of 'Overseer of the Pyramid-town of Khufu and Menkaure'; the tomb of **Idu**, the 'Scribe of Royal Documents'; and that of **Prince Khufukhaef**, who was 'Chancellor and son of Khufu.' The west cemetery also has some tombs open to the public. Two well worth visiting

are the tomb of **Iasen**, 'Overseer of the Guests of the Great House,' and the tomb of **Kaemankh**, 'Inspector of Prophets.' Both these tombs are decorated with fine tempera paintings executed on the smoothed plaster surfaces of the walls. The motifs include scenes of farming and fishing, and of the preparation of food and drinks. Rural life, agriculture, and livestock raising are also the main motifs of the paintings decorating the tomb of **Iymery**, 'Prophet of Khufu and Overseer of the Great House,' which

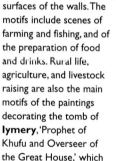

Idu, 'Scribe of Royal Documents'

lies in the southwest corner of the west cemetery. South of the Pyramid of Khufu, exactly opposite its southeast corner, is a beautiful chapel with a two-column vestibule: this is the tomb of **Seshemnepher**, a high official who lived around the end of the 5th Dynasty. Further south, beyond the Pyramid of Khafre, there is a small group of rock-cut tombs, two of which can be visited: the tombs of the overseer **Debhen** and of the vizier **Yun-min**, both of whom lived during the time of Menkaure.

The chapel of Seshemnepher

Saqqara

Situated on a rocky plateau on the west bank of the Nile, about ten kilometers south of Giza, Saqqara was the most important necropolis of Memphis, the capital of ancient Egypt. It was here that the first pyramid in Egyptian history was built.

The central section of the archaeological precinct at Saqqara, with Djoser's Step Pyramid

A short distance to the south of Giza lies the extensive necropolis of Saqqara, which has the large mastaba tombs of some 2nd Dynasty pharaohs as well as of 1st and 2nd Dynasty high officials. It was precisely at Saqqara that *Horus Netjerykhet*, better known as Djoser, decided to build his tomb, which was the first pyramid in Egypt. The site continued to house the Memphite pharaohs' tombs in the 5th and 6th Dynasty, and then in the 18th Dynasty, during the New Kingdom, when the capital was moved to Thebes, it was also used for the tombs of high officials such as Maya, Tutankhamun's treasurer, and Horemheb, the general who later ascended the throne of Egypt. Saqqara was not a necropolis only for humans; here in the immense burial ground known as the Serapeum, were the tombs of the Apis bulls sacred to the god Ptah, the principal Memphite divinity. In addition, mummified ibises, baboons, and cats were buried in the large galleries in the northern

One of the archaic 1st Dynasty mastabas

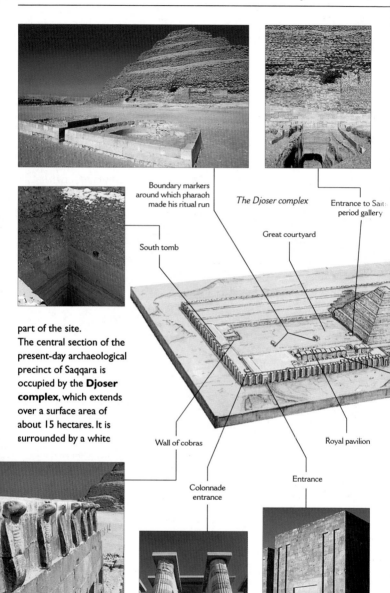

Boundary markers around which pharaoh made his ritual run

The Djoser complex

Entrance to Saïte period gallery

South tomb

Great courtyard

Royal pavilion

Wall of cobras

Colonnade entrance

Entrance

part of the site.

The central section of the present-day archaeological precinct of Saqqara is occupied by the **Djoser complex**, which extends over a surface area of about 15 hectares. It is surrounded by a white

Tura limestone enclosure wall, characterized by the so-called palace-façade paneling decoration that is believed to be an imitation of the wall of Memphis.

The Djoser complex, dominated by the **Step Pyramid**, includes many other architectural structures: the **South**

Tomb, which was probably connected to the cult of the pharaoh's *ka*, like the pyramid satellites that made their

appearance in the 4th Dynasty, and the **heb-sed court**, decorated with a double series of chapels and by two other structures known as the **Pavilion of the North** and **Pavilion of the South.** This section of the complex of Djoser was linked to the

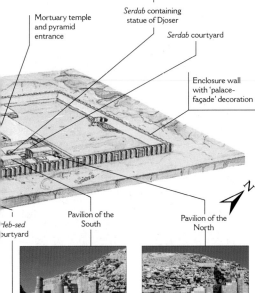

Mortuary temple and pyramid entrance

Serdab containing statue of Djoser

Serdab courtyard

Enclosure wall with 'palace-façade' decoration

Heb-sed courtyard

Pavilion of the South

Pavilion of the North

celebration of the pharaoh's *heb-sed* festival, held during his thirtieth year of rule. This was a symbolic renewal of his

physical power by means of a ritual run in the great courtyard on a course delimited by two **boundary markers** that

still exist. In like manner, in the chapels in the *heb-sed* court that were used for this purpose, there was a symbolic coronation of the pharaoh as ruler of Upper and Lower Egypt. Also, during this ceremony he received tribute from the various districts of his domain in the Pavilion of the South and Pavilion of the North. West of the Pavilion of the North, next to the mortuary temple that also lies on the north side of the Step Pyramid, is the **serdab**, a typical chamber in a mastaba tomb, in which the famous statue of the pharaoh Djoser was discovered; this sculpture was replaced by a copy and is now kept in the Egyptian Museum, Cairo.

Chapels

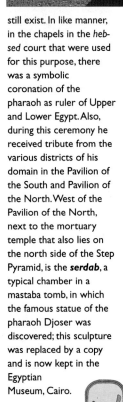

The cartouche of Djoser

Djoser's Step Pyramid

*A*ccording to tradition, the royal architect Imhotep invented the first pyramid, Djoser's Step Pyramid, which is the most impressive monument in the Saqqara necropolis.

Statuette of Imhotep (Archaeological Museum, Milan)

Aerial view of Djoser's Step Pyramid showing its west and south sides

*A*t first, Imhotep had conceived a large mastaba for his king, Horus Netjerikhet (Djoser), built over a shaft about 30 meters deep. This latter was connected to the burial chamber for the king's sarcophagus, to a series of chambers used to store the funerary equipment, and to eleven other burial shafts 32 meters deep situated on the east side of the structure and used for the pharaoh's consorts and sons. Later on, this initial mastaba was enlarged on its western side with the construction of four levels, or 'steps.' A few years later Imhotep decided to add two other steps, thus creating a sort of celestial staircase by means of which the pharaoh's *ka* (his immaterial double, or spirit) could be reunited with his father Re. The original entrance to the pyramid was on the north side, on the spot

Section of the Step Pyramid at Saqqara

First addition

Second addition

King's apartment with the blue-tiled chamber

Initial mastaba

Burial shaft

Burial shafts and galleries for pharaoh's consorts and sons

E   W

Burial chamber

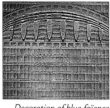

Decoration of blue faïence tiles from the king's apartment (Egyptian Museum, Cairo)

Cutaway showing the Step Pyramid

can be seen in the middle of the south side of the pyramid—that gave access to the central burial shaft. Djoser's pyramid was excavated and studied by the French architect and archaeologist Jean-

amazing quantity of objects—thousands of alabaster vessels lying in the underground chambers of the pyramid.

Jean-Philippe Lauer (1901-2001)

Height: 60 m

Entrance

Robbers' passage

Entrance of the initial mastaba, covered by the first addition

Burial shaft

Magazine galleries

Magazine galleries

Descending corridor

Magazine galleries

King's apartment

King's burial chamber

where a mortuary temple, a structure dedicated to the cult of the deceased king, was built (in later pyramids this structure was placed on the east side of the pyramid so that the pharaoh could benefit from the energy generated by the sun's rays at dawn). Despite the precautions taken and the expedients employed to make Djoser's tomb inviolate, the pyramid was profaned in ancient times. Indeed, during the 26th Saitic Dynasty, a long diagonal passage was hewn out of the rock— the entrance of which

Philippe Lauer, who began to work on this site in 1927 and continued for 70 years, thus effecting the scientific restoration and reconstruction of the complex of monuments around the Step Pyramid, such as the *heb-sed* court and chapels and the large colonnade entrance. Lauer's excavations brought to light an

The statue of Djoser found in the serdab *next to the mortuary temple, now in the Egyptian Museum, Cairo*

The Pyramid of Teti

The cartouche of Teti

Although in a rather poor state of preservation externally, the Pyramid of Teti, the first pharaoh of the 6th Dynasty, has perfectly intact mortuary chambers decorated with hieroglyphs of the Pyramid Texts.

The remains of the Pyramid of Teti seen from the east, with the ruins of the satellite pyramid

The Pyramid of Teti, which lies a few hundred meters northwest of the Step Pyramid, is a typical example of the architectural evolution these monuments underwent during the 5th Dynasty, characterized by a marked reduction in size (Teti's pyramid is 'only' 45 meters high), a parallel development in the mortuary temple and, from the reign of Unas

The inner chambers of the pyramid: the Pyramid Texts are inscribed in vertical registers on the walls

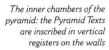

onward, by the appearance of the Pyramid Texts on the walls of the chambers. These texts are particularly well preserved in the Pyramid of Teti, the only exception being the burial chamber, the end of which is dominated by a gigantic sarcophagus made of *bekhen*, or greywacke, a stone from the Arabian Desert.

Detail of the hieroglyphs with the so-called Pyramid Texts; in the center is the cartouche with the pharaoh's name

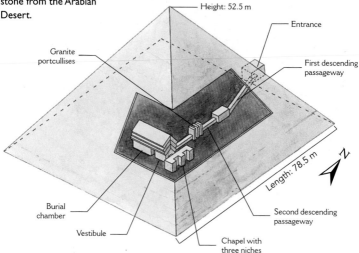

Height: 52.5 m

Entrance

Granite portcullises

First descending passageway

Length: 78.5 m

Burial chamber

Second descending passageway

Vestibule

Chapel with three niches

Section of the Pyramid of Teti

As was said above, the outer structure of the pyramid is quite deteriorated, since for centuries the monument was used as a quarry for building material. In fact, the mortuary temple was actually demolished as early as the Second Intermediate Period, that is, 600 years after its construction. At the southeast corner of the pyramid, next to the ruins of the mortuary temple, are the remains of a small satellite pyramid. Teti's successors (Pepy I, Pepy II, and Merenra) abandoned this section of the necropolis and built their pyramids further south.

The burial chamber with the large sarcophagus at one end

THE PYRAMID TEXTS

This is the name given to the collections of magical-religious texts with formulas and incantations that made their appearance at the end of the 5th Dynasty. They are inscribed in the inner chambers of the pyramids to help the soul of the deceased pharaoh ascend to heaven and become united with their celestial father Re.

The Pyramid of Unas

*T*he pyramid built for Unas, the predecessor of Teti and last 5th Dynasty pharaoh, is the smallest of the Old Kingdom pyramids, but was the first one in Egyptian history to have texts inscribed in it.

The Pyramid of Unas seen from the southwest, with the remains of the mortuary temple

*T*he Pyramid of Unas has marked architectural similarities with the Pyramid of Teti

The burial chamber

and, like this latter, has a very deteriorated exterior. It was in a bad state as early as the Ramessid age (19th Dynasty), a thousand years after it had been built. So Prince Khaemwaset, one of Ramesses II's sons, restored the outer casing and also had an inscription carved that recorded what may very well be considered the first restoration in history, naturally also mentioning the name of the legitimate owner of the monument.

The large mortuary temple is also in a poor state of preservation, but one can still recognize its most important elements. North of this building are two large mastabas belonging to Unas' queens, Nebet and Khenut, while to the south are the remains of the satellite pyramid. An impressive and well preserved 750–meter **causeway** goes from the mortuary temple to the valley temple a few dozen meters from the ticket office of the archaeological precinct. This causeway, which follows the course of a small valley, was decorated with finely-wrought bas-reliefs, some of which have been left *in situ*. The inner chambers of the **pyramid** are perfectly intact. They consist of a first descending passageway followed by another one, in which three granite portcullis slabs were

The causeway, with the granite jambs of the gate that Teti built in a later period

placed to block access, that leads to the antechamber. This latter affords access to both the burial chamber to the west and to a tripartite chapel to the east that was used to house the statues of the royal *ka* or the funerary equipment. The ceiling of the burial chamber, which is 7.3 meters long and 3.8 meters wide and on the west side of which is the large diorite sarcophagus of Unas, consists of two huge inclined limestone slabs decorated with a multitude of stars symbolizing the vault of heaven.

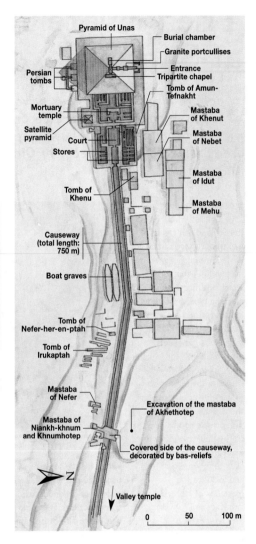

Pyramid of Unas
Burial chamber
Granite portcullises
Persian tombs
Entrance
Tripartite chapel
Tomb of Amun-Tefnakht
Mortuary temple
Mastaba of Khenut
Satellite pyramid
Mastaba of Nebet
Court
Stores
Mastaba of Idut
Mastaba of Mehu
Tomb of Khenu
Causeway (total length: 750 m)
Boat graves
Tomb of Nefer-her-en-ptah
Tomb of Irukaptah
Mastaba of Nefer
Excavation of the mastaba of Akhethotep
Mastaba of Niankh-khnum and Khnumhotep
Covered side of the causeway, decorated by bas-reliefs
Z
Valley temple
0   50   100 m

The remains of the valley temple, which originally stood on the edge of a canal connected to the Nile, are at the entrance of the archaeological precinct

The Private Tombs at Saqqara

*S*aqqara also has numerous private tombs, many of which are decorated with exquisitely beautiful bas-reliefs that are considered masterpieces of Old Kingdom art.

Ty, 'Overseer of the Pyramids of Nyuserra and Neferirkara'

Many of the high officials who lived in the 5th and 6th Dynasty had the privilege of being buried in the Saqqara necropolis. Their tombs, which are mostly of the mastaba type, are often quite large and are decorated with marvelous bas-reliefs, most of them polychrome, which illustrate various aspects of daily life connected to the deceased's activities. The private tombs open to the public lie in three main groups. The first is near the Pyramid of Teti and includes the mastabas of Mereruka and Kagemni.

The **mastaba of Mereruka** is the largest private tomb in Egypt. It is in fact a family tomb

The main hall in the tomb of the vizier Mereruka, with the statue of the deceased in a niche

Tomb of Mereruka: bas-relief of gold being weighed

with a rather complex plan that consists of 32 chambers divided into three sections. The tomb was designed not only for Mereruka, who bore the title of 'Vizier and Overseer of the City,' but also for his wife Seshseshet, the daughter of the pharaoh Teti, and their son Meri Teti. Among the most important bas-reliefs in this tomb are those depicting a hippopotamus hunt in the marshes, the working of gold, jewelry-making, and farmwork in the fields. A few meters away is the **mastaba of Kagemni**, who was also a vizier (the equivalent of a modern-day prime minister) at the beginning of Teti's reign. Although it is smaller than the other

Ship-building scene in the tomb of Ty

mastaba, this tomb also has a rather complex plan and covers a surface area of about 1,000 square meters. Its bas-reliefs are even more beautiful than the ones in Mereruka's tomb; for the most part the motifs are hunting and

The vizier Ptah-hotep smelling a perfumed ointment

fishing in the marshes, as well as agricultural labors. Further west is a second group of mastabas that includes those of Ty and Ptah-hotep. Despite its small size, the **mastaba of Ty**, 'Overseer of the Pyramids of Nyuserra and Neferirkara' who lived in the 5th Dynasty, is considered the most beautiful in the necropolis by some experts: among the scenes depicted in the bas-reliefs on its walls are the famous ones depicting shipbuilding. The offerings hall

communicates with a *serdab*, in which archaeologists found a strikingly beautiful statue of the deceased that was taken to the Egyptian Museum in Cairo and replaced with a copy. A short distance away is the **mastaba of Ptah-hotep**, a 5th Dynasty vizier and magistrate who shared this tomb with his father Akhtihotep, who was also a vizier. The mastaba is divided into two sections separated by a central four-pillared hall: to the north is Akhtihotep's section and to the south is Ptah-hotep's, which has the most beautiful and elegant bas-reliefs, the main attraction of this tomb. Lastly, further south, in the so-called 'Unas precinct,' is a third group of tombs that are not so popular as the others but are very

interesting.
This group includes the **tomb of Khenu**, the **mastaba of Princess Seshseshet Idut**, the

Bird-raising scene, tomb of Nefer-her-en-ptah

mastaba of the Vizier Mehu, the **mastaba of Nefer-her-en-Ptah** (also known as the 'tomb of the birds'), the **rock-cut tombs of Nefer** and **Irukaptah** (called the 'tomb of the butchers'), and lastly the **mastaba of Niannkh-khnum and Khnumhotep**, two brothers who lived in the 5th Dynasty and bore the titles of 'Prophets of Re' and 'Heads of the Great House Manicurists.'

Cow-milking scene in the mastaba of Kagemni

Memphis

*T*he capital of ancient Egypt for over 1,000 years, a leading religious center and seat of the cult of the creator god Ptah, Memphis lay on the east bank of the Nile opposite the Saqqara necropolis.

The god Ptah

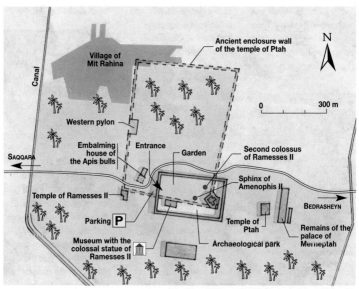

Plan of the archaeological precinct at Memphis

*A*ccording to the Greek historian Herodotus, Memphis was founded by the legendary king *Menes* (recently identified with Horus Aha), who unified Egypt and founded the 1st Dynasty at the beginning of the 3rd millennium B.C. The city, originally called *Ineb-hedj* ('the white wall') and later *Men-nefer*, or 'stability and

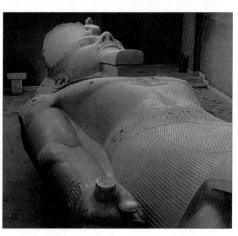

Colossal statue of Ramesses II at the Memphis Museum

Alabaster sphinx of Amenophis II

statue of Ramesses II that was discovered in 1820 by the Genoese traveler Giovanni Battista Caviglia. Other statues, such as the famous alabaster sphinx of Amenophis II discovered in 1912 by the great English archaeologist Sir William M. Flinders Petrie, who made the first important digs at this site, are in the adjacent garden. Outside the archaeological park the Egyptian Antiquities Service discovered, in 1951, the structures of the embalming **house of the sacred Apis bulls,** including an enormous alabaster embalming table

perfection,' after the name of the nearby Pyramid of Pepy I, was the political capital of Egypt during the entire Old Kingdom. Later on, when the capital was transferred to Thebes and then to Tanis in the Delta, Memphis maintained its position as the economic hub of the country as well as a major religious center, being the seat of the cult of the creator god Ptah; in fact, an enormous temple was dedicated to this divinity, the enclosure wall of which can still be distinguished. Today very little remains of the ancient city, whose original area has been covered by cultivated fields and a huge palm grove. The present-day archaeological area of Memphis—situated at the village of Mit Rahina, about 25 kilometers south of Cairo and about two km east of Saqqara—includes monuments and finds that for the most part date from the New

Kingdom. An **archaeological park** has a small **museum** almost entirely taken up by a colossal 12.8–meter

Alabaster embalming table for Apis bulls decorated with lions' heads

Detail of the decoration of the embalming table

decorated with lions' heads. The Apis bulls were considered incarnations of Ptah and sons of a virgin cow impregnated by the god himself. The bull was identified by the priests, lived in Memphis near the temple of Ptah, and enjoyed its special status until its death. During the New Kingdom the Apis bulls were buried in huge sarcophagi in the **Serapeum at Saqqara.**

The Pyramids of Dahshur

*O*pen to the public in 1996, the archaeological site of Dahshur, surrounded by the desert sand, is extremely interesting. It was here that Snofru, the founder of the 4th Dynasty, had the first true pyramid built.

The pharaoh Snofru

General view of Dahshur. In the foreground is Snofru's Bent Pyramid with its satellite pyramid, while the Red Pyramid can be seen in the background

Situated about ten kilometers south of Saqqara, Dahshur is the southernmost section of the Memphite necropolis. It was the site chosen by the pharaoh Snofru for the construction of the first true pyramid in history. It is unclear why this king, who also enlarged or finished the pyramid of Meidum, decided to build two other pyramids.

In any case, after the experiences of the 3rd Dynasty step pyramid, a concerted effort was made to build a true pyramid, the shape of which was probably more congruous with the new

The Bent Pyramid, also known as the South Pyramid

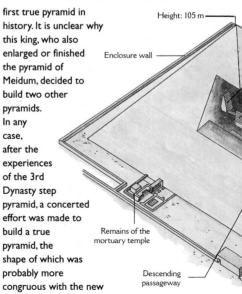

Height: 105 m

Enclosure wall

Remains of the mortuary temple

Descending passageway

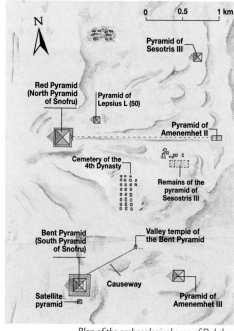

Plan of the archaeological area of Dahshur

known as the **Red Pyramid** because of the reddish limestone used for its construction, is the second largest pyramid in Egypt. Both of Snofru's pyramids at Dahshur have a complex inner layout, with three corbeled-ceiling chambers on different levels. Dahshur also has three **mudbrick**

The corbeled ceiling of the second chamber in the Red Pyramid

pyramids that were built in the Middle Kingdom; the most important and best preserved of these is the one belonging to the pharaoh Amenemhet III (12th Dynasty).

religious conceptions. Snofru's **Bent Pyramid** (or South Pyramid), originally 105 meters high, owes its name to the change in angle of slope, which went from 54° 27' 44" to 43° 22', probably owing to worrying signs of subsidence in the inner structures. Snofru's North Pyramid, better

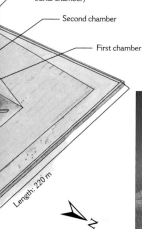

Third chamber (or burial chamber)

Second chamber

First chamber

Length: 220 m

Section of Snofru's Red Pyramid

The Red or North Pyramid of Snofru is the second largest in Egypt

The Pyramid of Meidum

*T*his pyramid, built in an isolated spot on the edge of the desert at the beginning of the Nile plain, about 50 kilometers south of Dahshur, has not yet revealed all its secrets.

The pyramid of Meidum surrounded by rubble

It is not known who actually built the pyramid at Meidum. It may have been Huni, the last pharaoh of the 3rd

The burial chamber in the pyramid, with its corbeled ceiling

Dynasty, or his son Snofru may have completed and modified the construction begun by his father. What is certain is that the pyramid was conceived as a step pyramid and that it was later transformed into a true pyramid with the addition of limestone slab casing; the later collapse of this dressing exposed the original core of the structure, producing the rubble that still surrounds the monument, which the locals call *al-haram-al kaddad*, 'the false

pyramid.' On the east side of the pyramid one can see a small **chapel**

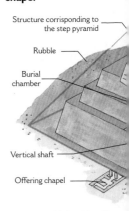

Structure corrisponding to the step pyramid

Rubble

Burial chamber

Vertical shaft

Offering chapel

Horizontal corridor with two recesses

New rooms found in 1998/200

The famous geese of Meidum, discovered in 1871 in the mastaba of Neferma'at, are rendered with such precision that the genus could be identified (Egyptian Museum, Cairo)

with two stelae that could be considered a mortuary temple in embryo. A large **causeway** descends from this chapel to the plain below amid the vegetation, while the valley temple has never been located. The **chambers in the interior**, which were first penetrated in 1881 by the famous French Egyptologist Auguste Mariette, are rather simple in structure, consisting only of a corridor and the burial chamber—which for the first time was built in the body of the pyramid and no longer in a shaft covered by the pyramid, as in the Step

The painted limestone statues of Prince Rahotep and his wife Nofret (Egyptian Museum, Cairo)

Pyramid at Saqqara. An important **private necropolis** was also discovered at Meidum. It housed the tombs of high 4th Dynasty officials and was excavated by Mariette and then, from 1909 to 1910, by the English Egyptologist William M. Flinders Petrie. In the necropolis tombs these archaeologists found masterpieces of ancient Egyptian art such as the statues of Prince

Section of the pyramid of Meidum

Rahotep, probably Snofru's son, and his consort Nofret, and the famous painting in the nearby mastaba of Neferma'at depicting a group of six geese that have been identified as two species belonging to the genera *Anser* (A. albifrons and A. fabalis) and *Branta* (B. ruficollis).

THE LASTEST DISCOVERY

From May 1998 to September 2000 the French archaeologists Gilles Dormion and Jean-Yves Verd'hurt, under the auspices of the Supreme Council of Egyptian Antiquities and with the aid of a microprobe and an endoscope, discovered two new chambers in the pyramid, each measuring 19 cubic meters, and two corridors whose function is for the moment unknown. The chambers lie right above the two small porticoes in the horizontal corridor. In March 2000 a third corridor was discovered: it begins at the second chamber and is oriented to the north.

Original height: 93.5 m

Part of the pyramid visible today, 68.5 m high

Rubble

Entrance

16,5 m

Length: 144 m

Descending corridor

ESSENTIAL BIBLIOGRAPHY

Clayton, P. A. *Chronicle of the Pharaohs.* London, 1994.
Edwards, I. E. S. *The Pyramids of Egypt. London,* 1972.
Fakhry, A. *The Pyramids.* Chicago and London, 1969.
Lauer, J. Ph. *Le mystère des pyramides.* Paris, 1988.
Lauer, J. Ph. *Saqqara. The Royal Cemetery of Memphis.* London, 1979.
Lauer, J. Ph. *Histoire monumentale des pyramides d'Egypte.* Cairo, 1962.
Lehner, M. *The Complete Pyramids.* Cairo, 1997.
Porter, B., R. L. B. Moss. *Topographical Bibliography of Ancient Egyptian Hieroglyphic Texts, Reliefs and Paintings.* Oxford, 1927–52, 1960.
Siliotti, A. *Belzoni's Travels.* London, 2001.
Siliotti, A. *Egypt: Temples, Men, and Gods.* Cairo, 2001.
Siliotti, A. *The Discovery of Ancient Egypt.* Cairo, 1998.
Siliotti, A. *The Pyramids.* Vercelli, 1997.
Stadelmann, R. *Die Ägyptischen Pyramiden—Vom Ziegelbau zum Weltwunder.* Mainz am Rhein, 1991.

PHOTOGRAPH CREDITS